Charles Ira Bushnell

A Narrative of the Life and Adventures of Levi Hanford

A Soldier of the Revolution

Charles Ira Bushnell

A Narrative of the Life and Adventures of Levi Hanford
A Soldier of the Revolution

ISBN/EAN: 9783337133511

Printed in Europe, USA, Canada, Australia, Japan

Cover: Foto ©ninafisch / pixelio.de

More available books at **www.hansebooks.com**

LEVI HANFORD

A

NARRATIVE

OF THE

LIFE AND ADVENTURES

OF

LEVI HANFORD,

A

SOLDIER OF THE REVOLUTION.

BY

CHARLES I. BUSHNELL.

NEW YORK:
PRIVATELY PRINTED.
1863.

TO

MY ANTIQUARIAN FRIENDS

AND TO

STUDENTS OF AMERICAN HISTORY GENERALLY

THIS VOLUME IS RESPECTFULLY

DEDICATED.

INTRODUCTION.

VERY few of the present generation appreciate the sufferings and sacrifices which were made by our forefathers in the war of the Revolution. While we enjoy the blessings which have descended to us, we little think of the immense cost at which they have been obtained. Those gallant, patriotic men, to whose noble and unselfish efforts we owe our present happiness and prosperity, are eminently worthy, and ought ever to receive our warmest admiration, gratitude and love.

It is for the purpose of perpetuating the memory of one of these noble soldiers that the following memoir is printed. Serving through the entire period of the war of the Revolution, it was his lot to endure more hardships and privations than is usual to fall to the lot of man. Although the trials he met with were many and severe, yet he bore them all with patience and fortitude, contenting himself with the patriotic reflection that his loss would be his country's gain.

In the following narrative will be found a particular account of the dangers he passed through and the sufferings he endured. Known too long and too well ever to be charged with or even suspected of the least approach to duplicity or deception, every reliance can be placed upon the truth of the statements it contains.

In the Appendix are added some explanatory notes, elucidating the text, to which the attention of the reader is directed. In conclusion, we would here express our acknowledgments to William B. Hanford, Esq., the son of the subject of the memoir, for the materials from which the present pamphlet has been compiled.

NARRATIVE.

LEVI HANFORD was the son of Levi Hanford, (¹) a respectable farmer of Norwalk, (²) Connecticut; and the maiden name of his mother was Elizabeth Carter. They were the owners of good farms and mills. They were pious Christians, sincere and devout, and were, for many years preceding their death, strict members of the Baptist Church. Mr. Hanford was a man of good mind, but of a quiet and domestic turn. He was the lineal descendant of Rev. Thomas Hanford,(³) a Congregational clergyman, who emigrated to this country from England about the year 1642, and settled in Norwalk, where he was, for some forty years, the established minister.

The subject of this memoir was born in Norwalk,
on the 19th day of September, 1759. He had two
brothers, one older and the other younger than
himself. His eldest brother, Ebenezer, had poor
health during much of his life. His youngest
brother, John, upon arriving at sufficient age,
enlisted in the Continental service, in which he
remained to the termination of the war. He
was engaged in some of the hardest-fought battles of the Revolution, and was considered a good
soldier. He was brave and determined, and thor-
oughly reliable, and was therefore generally one of
those who were selected when any important or
daring duty was to be performed. There were two
sisters in the family; Polly, the youngest of whom,
died at an early age. Elizabeth, the eldest sister,
married Capt. Isaac Keeler,(4) who served in the
Continental army to the termination of the war.

There was little in the early history of Levi
Hanford worthy of record. The days of his childhood and youth were mainly spent at school, or
with his father, on the farm, or in the mill. The
advantages for education in those days, as compared
with the present time, were, at the best, but very

limited. Schools and academies were but few and far apart, and there being but very few public libraries, access to books was extremely difficult. Even among the literary and wealthy, the supply was but meagre. In addition to this, the troubles with the mother country broke in upon and entirely disarranged, if not destroyed, what little organization had before existed. It is not, therefore, to be wondered at that young Hanford, who like many others of that day, could only attend school during the winter months, being engaged in the summer and autumn in the occupations of the farm, made but slow progress in his studies, and that his early education was, therefore, but very limited. This loss, however, he afterwards retrieved to a great extent by constant study, and by reading and conversation acquired considerable general knowledge, so much so that he became, in after life, somewhat noted for his acquirements and general intelligence.

Although the mental training of young Hanford was deficient, this was not the case with his moral education. Brought up under the constant eye of his parents, who were eminently pious and devout, he received every attention, and under their care-

ful teachings and guided by their example, he early
acquired those moral and religious principles which
laid the foundation of his character, and governed
his acts through life. Towards his parents, his
thoughts were often turned in after years, as well
as in youth, holding and cherishing for them always
the strongest attachment, and never alluding to or
speaking of them but with the most reverent affec-
tion and regard.

Among the prominent traits which distinguished
young Hanford from his companions, were his un-
tiring perseverance and energy of character, enab-
ling him to overcome and triumph over obstacles
at which most men would stand appalled. Although
possessed of courage that was equal to any emer-
gency, yet in his disposition he was humane and
charitable, in his intercourse modest and unassum-
ing, and in his bearing meek, gentle, and conciliat-
ing. In addition to these qualities, he was endow-
ed by nature with a remarkable degree of coolness
and self possession which seldom, if ever, forsook
him even under the most trying circumstances.

In the month of September, 1775, Hanford arrived
at the age of sixteen, and was then eligible to per-

form military duty and bear the hardships of the camp. The battles of Concord([6]) and Lexington([6]) had been fought, and the bravery and valor of the American soldier fully proved and substantiated. The glorious capture of Ticonderoga([7]) had taken place. That strong fortress, hitherto deemed impregnable, had been surprised and had fallen, and the name of Ethan Allen([6]) and the praise of his Green Mountain boys([9]) was upon every tongue. The flower of the British army had been opposed. and British pride had been more than humbled upon the bloody field of Bunker Hill([10]). Twice had those haughty red-coats advanced to the assault, and twice had they been, by raw militia, ignominiously repulsed. No wonder then that pride sat upon every face, that joy filled every heart, and that shouts of triumph rang through the excited land.

Roused by the common feeling and stimulated by the example of those around him, but no more so than by the natural emotions of his own patriotic heart, Hanford was not long idle. He soon shouldered his gun, and in the year 1776 became enrolled in a company of minute-men under the command of his maternal uncle, Capt. John Carter([11]).

He was liable as one of such to be called upon
for service at a moment's notice, communicated
sometimes by arranged signals, such as the ringing
of bells, the firing of cannon, or the tap of the drum,
and sometimes, in cases of extreme necessity, by
expressmen, who rode at full speed in all directions
to summon them forth. These minute-men would
sally out, armed and equipped, all repairing to a
common rendezvous as fast as they received the
order, those going first who were first notified, and
the others following and falling in the ranks as they
arrived on the ground. His duties as a minute-man
were to keep guard along the coast of Long Island
Sound and its vicinity, to prevent the carrying on
of illicit trade, the landing of Tories, Cow-boys([12]),
and others on expeditions of plunder, to arrest
Tories and those who should attempt to join the
British, and in general to be ready to repel the
attack of any hostile party that might appear.—
Such attacks were about that time very frequent,
being generally made by squads who came from
Long Island in whale-boats, who, after plundering
and burning and destroying what they could, would
then flee back to a place of safety before a sufficient

force could be collected to punish their audacity.
—In addition to this kind of service, volunteers
were often called for, and Hanford would frequent-
ly enlist, sometimes for a few months, but oftener
for still shorter periods. In the spring of the year
1776, he with others was sent under the command
of General Lee([13]), for a few weeks' service, to New
York, to defend that city against an anticipated
attack from the enemy. Upon his arrival, he was
one of a detachment of men that was sent to Governor's Island([14]) for the purpose of breaking ground
there, and erecting fortifications. It was on a dark
and stormy night. Guards were placed around the
Island to keep a look-out for danger and prevent
surprise. Some British men-of-war were lying off
in the harbor. They mistrusted that there was
something going on upon the Island, and had accordingly sent off their small boats to reconnoitre.
These reconnoitering parties would row up as near
to the shore as they dared, and when they came
within hailing distance, the sentinel on shore would
hail them, and receiving no answer, would fire upon
them, upon which the crew would immediately haul
off, and make their appearance at some other place,

when the same results would again follow. In this manner the night was spent. On the following morning the men were withdrawn from the Island, and in the evening they were again returned to it and the work resumed. He was engaged in this manner during his stay in New-York, which lasted only about one month, at the expiration of which time he left the city and returned to his home.

In the month of October, 1776, Hanford enlisted in a troop of horse, commanded by Captain Seth Seymour([15]), whose duty it was to guard and protect the sea-coast.

On the thirteenth day of March, 1777, he together with twelve others of the troop, was detached as a guard and stationed at South Norwalk, Connecticut, at a place then called "Old Well." The night was dark and the weather inclement, and the officers in consequence, negligent in their duties. In the course of the evening they were entirely surrounded by a party of British and Tories, from Long Island, who came over in whale-boats, and the whole guard were taken prisoners, poor Hanford among the rest, he being at that time but an ignorant boy, a little over seventeen years of age([16]).

The prisoners were conveyed across the Sound to Huntington,(") from there to Flushing(") and thence to New-York. Upon their arrival in the city of New-York, they were incarcerated in the old Sugar House prison in Crown, now Liberty-street, near the Dutch Church, at that time used as a riding-school for the British light horse, but of late years converted to, and still used as the General City Post Office([19]).

The old Prison, which is now torn down, was a brown stone building, six stories high,—but the stories were very low, and the windows small and deeply set, making it very dark and confined. It was originally built for a sugar refinery, and had been previously used as such. Attached to it was a small yard, and the whole was enclosed by a high board fence, so that the general appearance of the building was extremely gloomy, and prison-like([20]).

Upon our entrance into this miserable abode, says Hanford, we found some forty or fifty prisoners, all of whom were in a most wretched, emaciated and starving condition. The number of these poor sufferers was constantly being diminished by sickness and death, and as constantly increased by the

accession of new prisoners to the number of four
hundred to five hundred. Our allowance of provisions was a scanty supply of pork and sea-biscuit—
so scanty that the quantity would be far from keeping a well man in strength. The food, moreover,
was anything else than of a healthy character.—
The pork was old and unsavory, and the biscuit
was such as had been wet with sea-water, and being damaged, was full of worms and very mouldy.
It was our common practice to put water into our
camp-kettle, then break up the biscuit into it, and
after skimming off the worms, to put in the pork,
and then, if we had fuel, to boil the whole together.
The indulgence of fuel was allowed to us only part
of the time. On occasions when it was precluded,
we were compelled to eat our meat raw and our
biscuit dry. Starved as we were, there was nothing in the shape of food that was rejected, or that
was unpalatable.

Crowded together within our narrow abode, with
bad air to breathe, and such food to eat, it was not
strange that disease and pestilence should prevail,
and that too of the most malignant character. I
had not been long confined before I was taken with

the small pox, and conveyed to the small pox hospital([21]). Fortunately, I had but a slight attack, and was soon enabled to return to the prison.— During my confinement, however, I saw cases of the most malignant form, several of my companions dying in that building of that horrible disease.— When I came back to the prison, I found that others of our company had been taken to the different hospitals, there to suffer and die, for few of them were ever returned. I remained in the prison for a while, until from bad air, confinement, and unhealthy diet, I was again taken sick, and conveyed to the Quaker Meeting Hospital, so called from its having been used as a place of worship by Christians of that denomination([22]).

I became insensible soon after my arrival, and the time passed by unconsciously untill I began slowly and by degrees to recover my health and strength, and was then permitted to exchange once more the hospital for the prison.

Upon my return to the Sugar House, I found that during my absence, the number of my companions had become still further reduced by sickness and death, and that those who survived were in a most

pitiful condition. It was really heart-rending to
see those poor fellows, who but a short time before
were in the bloom of health, now pale and thin,
weak and emaciated, sad and desponding, and apparently very near their final end. While the poor
prisoners were thus pining away by degrees, an influence was constantly exerted to induce them to
enter the Tory regiments. Although our sufferings were intolerable, and although we were urged
to embrace the British cause by those who had
been our own townsmen and neighbors, and had
themselves joined the Royal ranks, yet the instances
were very rare that they could induce any one of
those sufferers to hearken to their persuasions.—
So wedded were they to their principles, so dear to
them was their country, so true were they to their
honor, that rather than sacrifice them, they prefer-
red the scoffs of their persecutors, the horrors of
their dungeon, and in fact, even death itself.

On one occasion, I heard a great noise and uproar in the prison, accompanied by loud curses and
threats of vengeance. Upon inquiry, I learned
that the guard had been stoned while at his post
of duty, and that the prisoners were charged with

the offence. This act having been repeated on one or two subsequent occasions, the British Commander at length came into the prison yard with a body of men. He questioned the prisoners very closely, but could elicit nothing that would implicate any one. He then told the prisoners that if the act was again committed, and the aggressor not revealed, the guard should fire upon the prisoners, when the innocent would suffer with the guilty. The following day, while I was standing in the prison yard, I saw a person come to a third-story window of a neighboring house, and partially concealed behind a chimney, waited until the sentry on duty had turned his back and was marching from him, when stepping from his place of concealment so as to get the full use of his arm, he hurled a brick bat at the sentry, striking him in the back, and injuring him severely. The guard were in an instant turned out and marched to the prison yard. The gates were thrown open, and the guard stood ready to fire. There was now no time to be lost, so I at once communicated what I had seen. The gates were thereupon closed, and the guard marched to the building where the man had appeared. After a terrible uproar, with loud swearing and cursing, the guard at length retired with one or two prisoners in their custody. What became of them I never knew. Nothing concerning them was ever revealed to us. However, there were no more complaints made, after this, of the stoning of the sentry.

The sentries, as a body, were not only ungenerous and uncivil, but unfeeling and tyrannical, and committed many acts of wilful, wanton cruelty.— They considered anything short of death, to rebels, as humanity. This feeling was far more prevalent among the British than among the Hessians ; and hence, when the prisoners desired any favors, they deferred asking for them until the latter had the guard, which was two days out of every five. Occasionally, a humane man was on duty, but he was restrained from obeying his natural impulses through fear of the official power above him. The orders under which they acted were absolute and imperative, and a disobedience of command or a dereliction of duty were sure to be followed by severe and immediate punishment. I shall never forget a striking instance of this which occurred during my captivity here.

In the prison yard there was a large bar of pig-iron, which the prisoners, for pastime, would amuse themselves by throwing, and their contests for superiority would often be attended by considerable excitement. One day, while they were thus engaged, the sentry on duty, a stout, good natured man, after gazing for some time upon the performances of the prisoners, became at length emulous of their efforts, and, upon the impulse of the moment, ventured to enter the list and compete with them. Laying down his gun, he made one trial, and coming but little short of the best of them, was encouraged to try again. Throwing off his cartridge box and bayonet, he again grasped the bar, and though he did better than before, yet he still fell short. Stimulated by his success, and determined to gain his point, he now threw off his stock and coat. At this instant, an officer suddenly came in, and noticing the condition of the sentinel, said to him in a stern, authoritative tone, " *Walk this way, sir.*" They left the prison together, and we learned that for this breach of duty, the sentinel was sentenced to run the gauntlet and receive three hundred lashes.

On the following day, a company of men were drawn up in double line, facing each other, and in full view from the prison. Each man stood a little from his neighbor, and each was armed with a raw hide. When everything was ready, all the drummers of the regiment, beating the long roll([23]), entered the lines, followed by an officer, with a drawn sword under his arm, the point turning backward. Then followed the prisoner, having nothing on but his breeches, and behind him came another officer with a drawn sword. As the prisoner passed through the lines, each man in succession gave him a severe blow with his raw hide. After he had passed, he then had to turn back again and retrace his steps, and thus walk up and down until the whole number of lashes was given. On the outside of each line an officer marched opposite the prisoner, and if any act of favor was shown, or if any man gave the prisoner a less forcible blow than he could have done, the officer would strike him so severely with the flat of his sword that he would almost bring him to the ground.

Under this dreadful trial the prisoner at first walked firmly and erect, but he soon began to

queck and droop, then to writhe and convulse, until
at length his lacerated body was thrown into con-
tortions, and was literally streaming with blood.—
Sometimes he would receive a blow upon his breast.
then upon his back, and then upon his head or legs,
according as his body happened at the time to be
placed. The scene was one of most barbarous
cruelty, and ended, as might well be supposed, in
the miserable death of the poor, offending sentinel.

Notwithstanding the sufferings we endured, and
the rigorous treatment to which we were subjected
in the prison, we were not without some friends
and sympathizers. Among these, there was a lady,
a Mrs. Spicer, who resided in the city, and who was
a warm friend to the cause of liberty. She took a
deep and lively interest in the condition of the
prisoners, and visited the hospitals and prisons
almost daily. She was esteemed by the prisoners
as a mother, and her visits anxiously looked for,
and received, always, w.th a warm and hearty welcome. She came, not alone, with the clear, mild
sunshine. She came with the howling storm, and
the whistling wind, and the pelting rain. The risk
of contagion and death, even, could not deter her

from her noble, saint-like mission. She came as a
ministering angel, comforting the sick, sympathiz-
ing with the distressed, and performing many acts
of kindness and mercy.

What became of her, or where she lived, I never
could learn. I made many efforts, after the war,
to ascertain, but never with success. Although
she has long since passed away, and her acts were
unknown to public ear, yet many a poor prisoner
has poured forth his blessings upon her. The
memory of that stranger's kindness will live in
many a heart until life's last pulse shall cease to
beat. Her deeds of mercy, though unrequited
here, have not been lost. They have been record-
ed in a higher sphere, where she will receive a
great and glorious reward.

I remained in the prison until the twenty-fourth
day of October, when the names of a company of
prisoners, mine among the rest, were taken down.
We were informed that the time had arrived for us
to return to our homes. We became, at once, ela-
ted at the prospect of a speedy release. Our feelings immediately started up from the depths of
despair. We joyfully drew our weekly provision,

and cheerfully divided it among our starving associates, from whom we were so soon to take our
leave. But, alas! little did we dream what a cruel
destiny was in store for us. How bitter, how ag-
gravating to us was the disappointment when we
found that, instead of being returned to our homes,
we were to be removed only to undergo still further torments. We were put on board the prison-
ship Good Intent([21]), then lying in the North River,
and reported there with one week's provisions.

The scene of starvation and suffering that followed, it is impossible to conceive, much less to describe. Crowded together as we were with over
two hundred in the hold of the ship, the air was
exceedingly foul, close, and sickening. Everything
was eaten that could possibly appease hunger.—
From these and other causes, and enfeebled as we
had become, and reduced as we were by famine, no
wonder that pestilence in all its fury began to sweep
us down. To such an extent did this prevail that
in less than two months' time our number was reduced by death to scarcely one hundred. In addition to all this we were treated with the utmost
severity and barbarity. Even the smallest indul-

gence was most rigidly denied. In the month of
December following, the river began to freeze,
when, fearing some of the prisoners might escape
upon the ice, the ship was moved round to the
Wallabout, where lay also the Jersey, another pri-
son-ship of horrific memory, whose rotted hulk still
remained, till within a few years past, to mark the
spot where thousands of brave and devoted martyrs
yielded up the precious offering of their lives, a
sacrifice to British cruelty(25).

Here again, I became sick, and my name was
again taken down for the hospital. The day before
New Year's, the sick were brought out, and placed
in a boat to be conveyed to the city. The boat
had lost a piece of plank from her bottom, but the
aperture was filled up with ice ; we were taken in
tow and proceeded on our course. The motion of
the water soon caused the ice to loosen, and our
boat began to leak. We had gone but a short distance when the sailors inquired " *whether we leak-
ed.*" Our men, either from pride, or from an un-
willingness to betray fear, replied, " *but a mere
trifle.*" The sailors, however, soon perceived our
increased weight. They pulled hard for a while,

and then lay to until we came up with them. Our
boat was at that time half filled with water. When
the sailors perceived our condition, they vented
their curses upon us, and with horrid oaths and
imprecations, pulled for the nearest dock, shouting
for help. When the boat reached her destination,
she struck level with the water, and we were compelled to hold on to the dock and to a small boat
by our side, to prevent her from sinking.

It being low water, the sailors reached down
from the dock, and clenching our hands, drew us up
in our turn. I well remember that I was drawn up
by them with such violence that the skin was taken
from my chest and stomach. One poor fellow, who
was unable to sit up, we had to haul upon the gun-
nel of the boat to keep his head out of water. Notwithstanding this, he still got wet, and died in a
few minutes after he was placed on shore.

From the boat we were taken to the Hospital in
Beekman-street, known as Dr. Rogers', afterwards
Dr. Spring's Brick Meeting House([26]). While pass-
ing through the yard, I took up one end of a bunk
from which some person had just been taken, dead.
I carried it into the church, and threw myself upon

it, perfectly exhausted and overcome. The head nurse of the hospital, passing by, saw and pitied my situation. She made me some warm tea, and pulling off the blankets from the poor, sick Irish, regardless of their curses and complaints, piled them upon me until I began to sweat profusely, and fall asleep.

The females who acted as nurses in the hospitals were many, perhaps most of them, the wives of British soldiers. Although they committed no designed acts of cruelty, yet many of them showed in their treatment of us much indifference and neglect.

When I awoke in the morning, some mulled wine and water was given to me. Wine and some other things were sent to the sick by our government.— As for the British, they furnished nothing. After taking the wine, I became refreshed. I lay perfectly easy, and free from pain. It seemed to me that I had never been so happy before in my life, and yet I was still so weak that I could not have risen from my bunk unaided even though it had been to "*save the union.*"* The doctor in attendance was an American surgeon, who had been taken prisoner.

* This was Hanford's own expression.

He had been taken from the prison and transferred to the hospital to attend the sick. Upon examining me, he told me that my blood was breaking down and turning to water, from the effect of the small pox, and that I needed some bitters. I gave him what money I had, and he prepared me some, and when that was gone, he was good enough to supply me some more at his own expense. Under his kind treatment and professional skill, I began slowly, and by degrees, to regain my strength, and in course of time, was once more able to walk about.

While standing, one day, in the month of May, by the side of the church, in the warm sun, my toes began to sting and pain me excessively. I showed them to the surgeon when he came in, and he laid them open. They had been frozen, and the flesh had become so wasted away that only the bone and the tough skin remained. I had, in consequence of my feet, to remain in the hospital for a long time, and of all places, that hospital was least to be coveted. Disease and death reigned there in all their terror. I have had men die by the side of me in the night, and have seen fifteen dead bodies, at one time, sewed up in their blankets and laid in the corner of the yard, the product of one twenty-four hours. Every morning, at eight o'clock, the dead cart came, and the bodies of those who had died the day previous were thrown in. The men drew the rations of rum to which they were entitled, and the cart was driven off to the trenches of the fortifications, where they were hastily covered, I cannot say interred.

On one occasion, I was permitted to go with the guard to the place of interment, and never shall I forget the scene that I there beheld. They tumbled the bodies promiscuously into the ditch, sometimes even dumping them from the cart, then threw upon them a little dirt, and away they went. I could see a hand here, a foot there, and there again a part of a head, washed bare by the rain, and all swollen, blubbering, and falling to decay. I need not add that the stench was anything but tolerable([27]).

The use of my feet having become restored to me, I was again returned to the prison in Liberty-street, and from this time forward, I enjoyed comfortable health to the close of my imprisonment, which took place in the month of May following.—

One day, while I was standing in the yard, near the high board fence which enclosed the prison, a man passed by, in the street, and coming close to the fence, without stopping or turning his head, said in a low voice, " *General Burgoyne is taken with all his army. It is a truth. You may depend upon it.*"(26) Shut out, as we were, from all information, and all knowledge of what was going on around us, this news was grateful to us indeed, and cheered us greatly in our wretched abode. Kept in entire ignorance of everything occurring beyond the confines of our miserable prison, we had been left to the most gloomy fears and forebodings as to the result of our cause. We knew not whether it was still progressing, or whether resistance had ceased altogether. Of the probability of our government being able to exchange or release us, we knew nothing. What little information we received, and it was very little, was received only through the exaggerations of British soldiery, and could, therefore, be but very little relied upon. How grateful then to us was the news which we had just heard—how sweet to our ears, how soothing to our hearts! It gave us the sweet consolation that our cause was still triumphant, and cheered us with the hope of a speedy liberation. It is fortunate, however, that our informant was not discovered, for if he had been, he would most probably have been compelled to have run the gauntlet, or to have lost his life for his kindness.

One day, I think it was about the first of May, two officers came into the prison. One of them was a sergeant by the name of Wally([20]), who had, from some cause or other, and what I never knew, taken a deep dislike to me. The other was an officer by the name of Blackgrove. They told us that there was to be an exchange of those prisoners who had been the longest confined, and thereupon they began to call the roll. A great many names were called to which no answers were given. Their owners had already been exchanged by that Being who has the power to set the captive free. Here and there was one left to respond. At last my name was called. I attempted to step forward and answer, when Sergeant Wally turned, and frowning upon me with a look of demoniac fury, motioned me to fall back. I dared not answer, so all was still. Then other names were called. I felt that, live or die, now was the time to speak. I accordingly told officer Blackgrove, that there were but eleven men present who had been longer in prison than myself. He looked at me, and then asked me why I did not answer when my name was called. I told him that I did attempt to answer, but Sergeant Wally prevented me. He thereupon turned, and, looking at him with contempt, put down my name. Of the thirteen who had been taken prisoners in the month of March, 1777, only two now remained to be exchanged, myself and one other([30]).

On the eighth day of May, 1778, we were released from our long confinement. Our persecutors, however, had not yet done with us. They, as if to trouble and torment us, took the Southern prisoners off towards Boston to be discharged, while the Eastern prisoners were conveyed to Elizabethtown, in New Jersey([31]). There they set us free. Upon our liberation, we preceeded at once to Newark.— Here, everything was clothed in the beauty of spring. The birds were singing merrily, and the whole face of nature smiled with gladness. We were so delighted, and in fact, so transported with pleasure, that we could not forbear rushing out and throwing ourselves upon the green grass, and rolling over it again and again. After a confinement of fourteen months in a loathsome prison, clothed in rags and filth, and with associates too numerous and offensive to mention, this was to us a luxury indeed.

From Newark(³²), we traveled on as fast as our enfeebled powers would permit. We crossed the Hudson at Dobb's Ferry(³³), and here we began to separate, each for his own home. The officers pressed horses and went on. My companion and myself were soon wending our way, slowly and alone. As we passed on, we saw in the distance two men riding towards us, each having with him a led horse. It did not take me long to discover the man on a well-known horse to be my father, and the other person to be the father of my comrade. The meeting I will not here attempt to describe, but from the nature of the case, you may well imagine that it was an affecting one, and more peculiarly so, as my friends had been informed some time before that I had died in prison. They had had prayers offered up, according to the custom of the time, and the family had gone into mourning(³⁴).

They therefore felt as though they had received me from the dead. It seems that the officers had carried the news of our return, and our friends had ridden all night to meet us. We proceeded on our way together, and ere the shades of evening had closed around us, we were once more in the bosom of friends, and enjoying the sweets of home, and the society of those we loved. And may my heart ever rise in gratitude towards that Being whose preserving care has been over me, and who has never, never forsaken me.

Hanford did not remain long idle after his return from imprisonment. As soon as he had regained his health, he resumed his musket, and partook once more of the hardships of the tented field.— He again took his position in Captain Seymour's company, and continued in the active performance of his duty to the termination of the war. He was present at the taking and burning of Norwalk, in Connecticut, and assisted in driving the British and Tories back to their shipping(**). At another time, he was one of a body of troops that was called out one cold winter night to repel a large British force that was advancing from Kingsbridge, forag-

ing, marauding, and burning everything in their
way([36]). The American army marched in two divi-
sions, one taking the Post-Road, and the other a
more circuitous route, and coming together at a
designated place near the enemy. The night was
excessively cold, and the army suffered greatly.—
The detachment to which Hanford belonged, arrived
first at the place of destination, and halted near a
public house. Hanford, and a few others of his
party, soon entered the house, and found their way
to the fire. While they were engaged in warming
themselves, an officer, whose name is not now re-
collected, came in, chilled and shivering with cold,
and placed his arms over Hanford's shoulders to
warm his hands, which were quite stiff and benumb-
ed. While thus engaged, he and Hanford were led
to notice each other, and with a mutual half recog-
nition. Soon after this, Hanford was stationed as
a guard at the outer door of the house, and while
performing this duty, the officer walked past him
repeatedly, each time eyeing him closely. Finally,
coming up to Hanford, he thus addressed him :—
" *Sir, I think I know you. I recognize you as one
of my fellow-prisoners of the old Sugar House Pri-*

*son in New-York. I thought I knew you when I
first saw you. I was with you for a while in that
den of human suffering.*" After a mutual greeting,
he asked Hanford how he liked his present position,
to which the latter replied that he was not particularly attached to it. The officer then asked him
how he would like to take a ride. Being answered
in the affirmative, the officer then told him that he
had letters and dispatches to the Secretary of
State, at Hartford([37]), Connecticut, and if he desired the trip, he would like him to go and deliver
them. He told him, moreover, that he must fur-
nish his own horse, pay his own expenses, and
when he had performed the duty, he must make
his report, when he should be re-imbursed and
draw his pay. To this Hanford readily assented.
The duty was accordingly performed by him, after
the return of the troops, and the trip to Hartford
was a pleasant one.

In the meantime, the troops passed on, and after
several skirmishes, and a running fight, the British
were finally driven back across Kingsbridge.—
About this time, a party of British and Hessians
commenced the erection of a redoubt on the Har-

lem river, and a body of men, of which Hanford
was one, was sent to check their operations. The
troops marched all night, intending to surprise the
enemy, and make the attack at early dawn. They
reached their destination before daylight, unob-
served, and took a position from which they could
rake the redoubt with their small arms, aided by
one piece of artillery loaded with grape. In front
of, and near the redoubt, was a vessel lying at the
dock, loaded with fascines([38]), a portion of which
had already been landed. The Americans were
hid from view when lying down, but when they
arose, the whole scene was open before them. At
daylight, a detachment of Hessian troops made its
appearance, and soon came to the water for fascines.
The Americans lay perfectly still until each Hessian soldier had shouldered his bundle, and was
about to return to the fort, when the command was
given in a loud tone of voice, " Attention, men—
—ready—aim—fire !" Quick as thought, each man
sprang to his feet, and a volley of musketry and a
discharge of grape were poured in upon the enemy.
The scene that followed was ludicrous in the extreme. The enemy were taken completely by sur-

prise, and were terribly frightened. In their confusion and terror, they threw down their bundles, and used every exertion to run. Although they jumped, and sprang, and swung their arms, and made desperate strides, yet they seemed for a time to have lost all ability to move forward, for when one leg started in one direction, the other went off in one exactly opposite ; and it was only by the most desperate efforts of springing and jumping that they effected their escape. This they were at last enabled to do by reason of the river being between them and their pursuers. The Americans, however, succeeded in carrying out the objects of the expedition. They destroyed the redoubt, made a prize of the vessel and cargo, and captured some prisoners.

On another occasion, when a party of British and Tories came on an expedition of plunder and destruction, Hanford was again called out, with others, to repel them. They met the enemy, and after a slight skirmish, succeeded in driving them back. The Americans pursued the retreating foe until the engagement became a running fight. The British finally made a stand in a favorable position,

and when their pursuers came up, they found a
rising ground before them, partially concealing the
enemy from their view. A portion of the Americans,
Hanford among them, passed over the ridge, amid
a galling fire, the bullets flying among them thick
as hail. Hanford soon found shelter behind a large
rock, under cover of which he used his gun for
some time with telling effect, till finally, in attempting to load it, the cartridge stuck in the barrel, and
in striving to force it down with his rod, he inad-
vertently leaned back to gain more space, in doing
which, a part of his person became exposed to view.
At that instant, a ball came whizzing by, just missing his head, and looking up, he perceived a British soldier in the act of dodging back to his covert.
The Americans firmly maintained their ground, and
finally bore off the honors of the day. They
charged upon, and repulsed the enemy, who retreated in confusion to their lines.

After this, Hanford spent the remaining part of
his term of service in guarding property, in repel-
ling the invasions of the British and the Tories,
and in peregrinate movements wherever his duty
or the public exigency required, until the termi-

nation of the war. In this manner, he gave himself up to the call of his country, evincing at all times, and upon all occasions, those traits of character, which, when found in happy combination, form the true model of the Christian soldier. At the establishment of peace, he threw off the trappings of war, laid aside the implements of death, and sought once more the shades of private life.

In the year 1782, Hanford was united in marriage to Miss Mary Mead,(³⁹) a lady of most amiable and exemplary character, with whom he had long been acquainted, and who was the daughter of Gen. John Mead,(⁴⁰) of Horseneck,(⁴¹) in Greenwich,(⁴²) Connecticut. Mr. Hanford, after his marriage, settled in New Canaan, (⁴³) then a parish of Norwalk, where he resided for more than twenty-five years. During his residence in New Canaan, he went with his wife to Walton,(⁴⁴) Delaware County, New York, on a visit to her brother and sister who had moved to that place. They performed the journey on horseback, the only mode of travel at that day. They traveled over bad roads, through woods, and fording deep and rapid streams. In the fall of the year 1807, he again visited Walton, but this time,

with the intention of purchasing a farm, and se-
curing a residence. Upon his return, he sold his
property in Connecticut, and on the twentieth day
of March, 1808, with two wagons, loaded with goods,
and his family of five sons and four daughters, he
moved to Walton. The winter was past, the weather warm and pleasant, and the traveling reason-
ably good. After a toilsome journey of six days,
the family arrived at their place of destination.
They took possession of their plain, but comfortable home, a log house of ample accommodation, and
soon became settled in their new abode. Here
they remained, a happy and unbroken family, until
the fifteenth day of September, 1847, when Mrs.
Hanford closed her earthly pilgrimage, in the 88th
year of her age, having lived with, and cheered the
fireside of her husband for more than sixty-five
years.

In the early history of Walton, religious confer-
ence meetings were held in the town every Thurs-
day evening, under the superintendence of Deacon
St. John.([*]) They were held at private houses, in
alternate rounds. In these gatherings, Levi Hanford took a warm and active part, generally lead-

MRS. HANFORD

ing the meetings when Deacon St. John was absent.
These meetings exerted a great influence upon the
neighborhood, and kept many from deviating from
the paths of moral rectitude. To this day, there
are many persons, now scattered over our country,
who look back to them as the source from which
they derived much of their religious training. Encouraged by the clergy, and patronized by their
occasional presence, they have been kept up for a
period of nearly seventy years, although their lead-
ers and principal supporters have been changed
several times by death or removal.

In the month of January, 1852, an advertisement
appeared in the New York Journal of Commerce,
stating that the author, David Barker, Esq., of that
city, had in his possession a cane, made from one
of the beams of the Old Sugar House in Liberty
street, and calling upon any surviving sufferer in
that old prison, to send in his name that he might
have the pleasure of presenting the relic to him as
a support to his declining years. To this call, five
only responded, disclosing the melancholy fact that
of those prisoners, only five remained alive. Each
of these applicants sent in his name, with a brief

account of his imprisonment and sufferings. It appeared from these statements that Levi Hanford was confined the longest of the five, and was the youngest of the number when imprisoned. There being so many applicants for the cane, it was concluded to leave the choice to be determined by lot. When this decision was made known to Hanford, he at once gave up all hope of receiving it, saying that in all his life, he never had any fortune in chance operations. The drawing, however, came off, and the cane fell to Hanford. It was transmitted to him by a friend, and he received it in the ninety-fourth year of his age, with a deep feeling of pride and pleasure. So delighted was he with this memento of his early career, that he kept it always near him, occasionally exhibiting it to those who visited him, and cherishing and preserving it to the day of his death.

Mr. Hanford always took a deep and lively interest in his country's welfare. On the exciting subjects which so much affected the nation's well-being, he took sides with the Republicans. He was a strong opponent of the leading acts and measures of John Adams, and the party that elected him,

but he was a warm friend and supporter of Thomas
Jefferson, and his administration. His heart was
with the Republicans in resisting the aggressive
acts of Great Britain and France, in discarding
their claimed right of search, and in opposing their
Milan and Berlin decrees. He approved of the
war of 1812, and the policy of Madison, and gave
them his firm and steady support, and though age
had placed him beyond the period of active duty
himself, yet he gave three of his sons, all who were
then of age, to the defence of that country, for
which he himself had suffered so much, and which
he had helped to establish. His two eldest sons
were called to the Canadian frontier at Sackett's
Harbor, and the younger to the defense of New
York, when that city was threatened with an inva-
sion. When peace was again restored, and the
government strengthened and invigorated, and
rendered more permanent by the ordeal through
which it had passed, he rejoiced with the joyful,
gave thanks with the thankful, looking forward
with true, patriotic pride to that enviable position
which she would hereafter take among the nations
of the earth—a higher, a brighter, a nobler posi-

tion than she had heretofore attained. He gave
his hearty and unwavering support to Andrew
Jackson, and the measures of his administration,
regarding him as a man far above the leading poli-
ticians of his day, pure, honest and self-sacrificing,
striving for the good of the country with a firm
and fearless determination that allowed no claim,
no interest, no obstacle whatever to swerve him
from his duty. As a Democratic Republican, Hanford warmly and cheerfully espoused the general
principles of that party, but when Texas was presented for annexation, he felt that it was a measure
which might end with disastrous results. He considered it as detrimental to the public good, that
it was not sought for through any real sympathy
for Texas, but was urged solely with the view of
opening a new field for the ingress of slavery, and
of increasing thereby the value of such property
by increasing its demand. With Texas for a pre-
cedent, he always feared that annexation might be
carried to a dangerous extent, and often remarked
that if this Union was ever dissolved, the annexation of Texas would be the first link in the chain
of events to bring it about. Though never an abo-

litionist, in the common acceptation of the term, yet he was always opposed to slavery in every form, considering it as a disgrace to humanity, a blot upon the national character, and a withering curse upon those States where it existed. He was in favor of letting it die out gradually, as he considered it would have done if the annexation policy had not given it new life by breathing into it an increased pecuniary interest. For these reasons he was opposed to all measures tending to the repeal of the ordinance of 1787, and of the Missouri Compromise. He considered such measures equally detrimental to the interest and stability of our government. When Congress was legislating upon the repeal of the Missouri Compromise, he took a deep and lively interest in its discussions, and his feelings became unusually excited. The subject was one that seemed to call out and develop all the energy of his earlier years. One day, after he had received his paper, and had perused the congressional proceedings, he turned to his son, and with a look of deep and solemn earnestness, said :

" *William, I see clearly that they are determined to repeal the Missouri Compromise, and I believe they*

will do it. They seem determined to break down
every barrier to the spread of slavery—those barriers
which were established at the commencement of our
government, and which have hitherto been held as sacred as the Constitution itself. If," said he, "ruthless
hands are to be laid upon those sacred compacts, and
those barriers to be broken down, trampled upon, and
destroyed, then will the curse of slavery spread,—then
will tyranny and oppression reign triumphant o'er
the land. Little, alas! very little will we have gained
in our Revolutionary struggle, if these things come to
pass. We endured privations—hunger, cold, toil and
suffering to little purpose—we gave our treasure—we
shed our blood—we gave our lives—all for naught, if
these lines of demarkation are to be disregarded,
scorned and taken away. If those worse than parri-
cides, were so bent upon sapping the foundation upon
which our great and almost perfect government is
founded, and upon which its very life depends, why,
oh! why could they not have waited a little longer,
until the last of the old soldiers had passed away, and
spared them the pain, the bitter mortification of wit-
nessing that noble structure which they sacrificed so
much to rear, broken down and destroyed, and the na-

tion reeling and falling back to that state of tyranny which cost so much treasure and so much blood to overthrow."

Thus spoke that honest patriot, and as he closed, as if to give due emphasis to his remarks, he stamped his foot upon the ground, while his tremulous voice and earnest look evinced the depth of the emotions that convulsed his heart. Oh! could those political vampires have beheld that aged man, have seen his solemn and impressive mien, and heard his soul-inspiring words. Though seared be their consciences, though obdurate be their hearts, that scene might have touched some tender chord, aroused some latent principle to check those unprincipled legislators in their headstrong course of depravity and ruin.

In his religious belief, Mr. Hanford was a frank and hearty supporter of the doctrines of the Baptist Church. Though fixed in his theology, yet he was no bigot. He was never arrogant or dogmatical, never narrow or illiberal. While he held his own views with tenacity, he allowed others to do the same, and to hold theirs undisturbed. His heart was ever open in brotherly fellowship, and in all the relations of life, he ever manifested that true, humble, Christian spirit, of which any one might well be proud. He combined in his character the purity of a saint with the valor of a Roman, —a splendid model of the old Continental soldier, —a brave—a holy—"an honest man—the noblest work of God."

But age was fast doing its work. A life of activity, of industry, of temperance, of virtue, had already extended his years far beyond the usual bound. At last, exhausted nature gave way, and on the nineteenth day of October, 1854, at his residence in Walton, Delaware County, New York, in the ninety-sixth year of his age, he sank calmly to rest,

"Calmly as to a night's repose, ·
Like flowers at set of sun."

His remains were deposited by the side of his wife in the family cemetery at Walton, attended by a large circle of friends and relatives, to whom he had endeared himself in life, and by whom he was lamented in death.

Levi Hanford is dead, but yet he lives !—lives in the hearts of his children, to whom he has bequeathed his spotless name—lives in the memory ot his many acquaintances, who

" Knew him but to love him,
Who named him but to praise,"

—lives in the pure—the brilliant example which he has made and left behind him.

NOTES.

(1.) Levi Hanford, Sen., the father of the subject of this memoir, was born in Norwalk, Conn., in that part of the town which afterwards became New Canaan, on the 4th day of March, 1731. He died on the 21st day of November, 1796, at the age of 65 years, and was buried in the Congregational Church-yard, in New Canaan.

His wife, whose maiden-name was Elizabeth Carter, was born in Norwalk in the year 1731, and died on the 7th day of September, 1776, at the age of 45 years, and was interred in the same burial-place as her husband. Her father, Ebenezer Carter, was born near the village of Norwalk, and was a farmer by occupation. At an early age he moved with his parents to what was then called "The Woods,"—some four miles distant. The country was then new, and deer, bears, and other wild animals were very plenty. In the latter part of his life he used to amuse the children and young people by relating to them the events of his early childhood, when wild animals would cross his path in going to and returning from church. He was an active, energetic man, and was proverbial for his hospitality. He and his wife were both buried in New Canaan.

(2.) Norwalk, a town in Fairfield Co., Conn., on Long Island Sound, 63 miles from Hartford, and 45 miles from New York City. It has a good trade, and a number of vessels employed in coasting. There is a regular communication between this place and New York. Old Well is situated a little more than a mile from the centre of the town. It received its name from an *old well*, from which, in early times, vessels engaged in the West India trade took their supplies of water.

(3.) REV. THOMAS HANFORD, according to Cotton Mather, was one of the class of ministers, " who not having finished their education at home, came over here to perfect it, before our college was come to maturity to bestow its laurels." He was in Scituate, Mass., in 1643, with the Rev. Charles Chauncey, one of the most distinguished Puritan divines, with whom he probably completed his studies. Mr. Hanford was made a freeman in Massachusetts, on the 22d day of May, 1650, began to preach in Norwalk in 1652, was ordained in 1654, and died in the year 1693, aged about 72 years. He was succeeded by the Rev. Stephen Buckingham. The widow of Mr. Hanford died on the 12th day of September, 1730, at the age of one hundred years.

(4) CAPTAIN ISAAC KEELER was born in Wilton, Conn., in the year 1755. He was apprenticed to, and learned the tailor's trade. On the breaking out of the war, he entered the Continental Army as an ensign, and was promoted to Lieutenant, and afterwards to Captain. He was with the army at Valley Forge, and was at the battle of Red Bank, under Col. Green, and also in other engagements. At the end of the war, he went into business at Waterford, Saratoga Co., N. Y. He afterwards moved to the City of New York, where he opened a merchant tailor's store. He received the appointment of City Marshall, and held at one time the office of Police Justice. He afterwards

occupied a position in the Custom House, which he retained to
his death. In the war of 1812, when the City of New York was
in danger of an attack by the British, he volunteered in the vet-
eran corps of revolutionary soldiers, for three months to guard
the Arsenal, and received an appointment in the corps. Though
he endeavored to discharge his duties with fidelity, the labors and
exposures of camp life were too much for his years and enfeebled
constitution. He took a severe cold, which settled upon his
lungs, and ended in consumption, of which he died in the year
1825, in the 71st year of his age. His wife was burned to death
about three years afterwards, her clothes taking fire while kneel-
ing in secret prayer. She and her husband were both buried in
the burial-ground of the church in Market Street, in the city of
New York, of which church they were both members.

(5 & 6) With a view of seizing the military stores and provisions which the Americans had collected at Concord, 12 miles
N. W. from Boston, Gen. Gage, on the evening preceding the
19th of April, 1775, detached from his garrison 800 picked men,
under the command of Lieut.-Col. Francis Smith, of the 10th
Regiment, and Major John Pitcairn, of the Marines. These
troops made a rapid march to the place of their destination, in
hopes of taking the malcontents by surprise, but, notwithstanding the precautions which had been taken, the alarm was given
throughout the country, and the inhabitants flew to arms. Between 4 and 5 o'clock on the morning of the 19th, the advanced
guard of the Royal troops arrived at Lexington, where they
found about fifty or sixty, or possibly more, of the American
militia under arms, whom Major Pitcairn ordered to disperse,
and on their hesitating to obey his command, that officer discharged his pistol and ordered his soldiers to fire. By the volley which ensued, eight of the militia were left dead on the ground,
ten were wounded, and the remainder dispersed. The troops

then proceeded to Concord, six miles further, where they destroyed a portion of the stores of the insurgents, and then commenced
retreating towards Boston. They were not, however, permitted
to make this retrograle movement without molestation. Before
they-left Concord, they were attacked by the American militia
and minute-men whom they had provoked, and who accumulated
by degrees, harrassed their rear and flanks, taking advantage of
every inequality of ground, and especially availing themselves of
the stone walls which skirted the road, and which served them as
intrenchments. Had not the detachment been met at Lexington
by a brigade of about 1,000 men with two pieces of cannon
which Gen. Gage had sent out to its support, under the command of Lord Percy, it would certainly have been cut off, or
forced to surrender. The United British forces arrived, wearied
and exhausted at Bunker Hill near Boston, a little after sunset,
having not only lost their baggage wagons, but sustained a loss
of about 65 killed, 180 wounded, and 28 missing. Among the
wounded was Lieut.-Col. Smith, the commander of the detachment. Some of the soldiers were so much exhausted with fa-
tigue that they were obliged to lie down on the ground, their
tongues hanging out of their mouths like dogs after a chase.
The Americans had about 50 killed, 34 wounded and 4 missing.
Intelligence of the battle spread rapidly through the Colonies,
and excited everywhere feelings of mingled exultation, sorrow
and rage. The mechanic left his work-shop and the farmer his
plough, and seizing their arms, they resolved to avenge the
death of their murdered countrymen.

Gordon's Amer. War, Vol. I, p. 476.

(7) In the year 1775, the project was conceived of surprising
Ticonderoga, a fortified post on the western shore of Lake Cham-
plain, and commanding the entrace into Canada. This design
was communicated to Col. Athan Allen, who, in conjunction with

Col. Benedict Arnold, accordingly proceeded to Ticonderoga, and the remainder of the party to Skeensborough. Sentinels had been previously stationed on all the roads to prevent the passing of any intelligence. On the 9th day of May, about eighty, all that the boats could carry, crossed the lake and landed near the garrison. The two Colonels advanced along side of each other, and entered the gateway leading to the fort, by the grey of the morning. A sentinel snapped his fusee at Col. Allen and then retreated. The main body of the Americans then followed and drew up. Capt. De la Place, the Commander, was surprised in bed, and compelled to surrender the place. When the remainder of the party arrived, they were despatched under Col. Seth Warner, to take possession of Crown Point, and Arnold, hastily manning a schooner, sailed to capture a sloop-of-war lying at the outlet of the lake. These two expeditions, as well as that against Skeensborough, were successful, and thus was obtained, without bloodshed, the command of those important posts, together with more than 100 pieces of cannon, besides small arms, and other munitions of war, with stores, &c. The unexpected news of this brilliant success imparted high courage and animation to the Americans, and caused great joy and exultation.

Gordon's Amer. War., vol. II, p. 11.

(8) ETHAN ALLEN was born in Connecticut in 1738, and moved in early life to Vermont. He distinguished himself in the controversy in 1770 between the inhabitants of that State and the government of New York, and was declared by the latter an outlaw. At the commencement of the Revolution, he, with the inhabitants of Vermont, took a vigorous part in resisting the British. In May, 1775, at the head of a small party, he surprised and captured Ticonderoga. In the autumn of that year he went several times into Canada, to ascertain the disposition of the people, and endeavor to attach them to the cause of the Colonies.

In an attempt to take Montreal, at the head of a small body of troops, he was captured and sent to England. After a long and severe confinement, he was at length exchanged and returned to Vermont, and was appointed to command the militia of that State with the rank of Brig.-Gen., but was not called to any important service. He was a man of gigantic size, and possessed great strength. He had a strong mind, indomitable will and courage, but was without the polish of education. In his religious opinions he was a Deist. He died in Colchester on Feb 13, 1789, aged 51 years.

(9) The name of " Green Mountain Boys" was applied to those persons who resided within the limits of the Green Mountains in Vermont. They were a brave and hardy race of men, and were chiefly settlers from New Hampshire, Massachusetts and Connecticut.

(10) Fearing an intention, on the part of the British, to occupy the important heights at Charlestown and Dorchester, which would enable them to command the surrounding country, about 1.000 men were despatched on the evening of the 16th of June, 1775, under command of Col. Wm. Prescott, to Bunker Hill, with instructions to fortify that position. They were conducted by mistake to Breed's Hill, which was nearer to the water and to Boston than Bunker's. At 12 o'clock they began to throw up entrenchments, and by dawn of day had completed a redoubt about eight rods square. As soon as they were discovered, they were fired upon by a ship-of-war, and several batteries, but the Americans, nevertheless, continued to labor until they had nearly completed a slight breastwork extending eastward to the water. In the morning they received a reinforcement of five hundred men. The British were astonished and incensed at their temerity, and determined to drive them off. Accordingly, about noon, a

body of 3,000 regulars commanded by Sir William Howe, left Boston in boats, and landed in Charlestown, at the extreme point of the peninsula, where they formed and marched slowly up the hill. The Americans reserved their fire until the British were within ten or twelve rods of the redoubt, when, taking steady aim, they poured an incessant discharge upon them, doing great execution, and causing them to retreat in haste and disorder down the hill. Being stimulated by their officers, the British again formed in line, and were again induced to ascend. The Americans now reserved their fire until the enemy had approached even nearer than before, when a tremendous volley was at once poured among them, causing them to retreat with precipitation even to their boats. So great was the carnage, and such the panic, that Gen. Howe was left almost alone on the hill side, his troops having deserted him, and nearly every officer around him being killed. At this moment, Gen. Clinton arrived with a reinforcement, and by his exertions the troops were a third time rallied and were impelled forward by their officers, who marched behind them with drawn swords. The fire from the ships and batteries was now redoubled, and a few cannon had been so placed as to rake the breastwork from end to end. The Americans having exhausted their scanty supply of ammunition, defended themselves for a short time with the butt end of their muskets, but were soon compelled to retire from the unequal contest. This they did with the order and regularity almost of veterans. The British had suffered too severely to pursue them, and merely took possession of the hill. The British lost about 1,054 killed and wounded. Among the killed was Maj. Pitcairn, who was in the expedition to Concord and Lexington. The loss of the Americans was about 453 killed, wounded and missing. Among the killed was Gen. Warren, a man of marked ability and standing, whose death was deeply deplored. The Americans were commanded by Col. Wm. Prescott, of Pepperel, an officer of great prudence and of

most determined bravery. Though the Americans were compelled to yield the ground for want of ammunition, yet their defeat was substantially a triumph. Their conduct was such as
effectually wiped away the reproaches of cowardice which had
been cast upon them by their enemies in Britain. Though raw
militia, yet they had twice repulsed the flower of her army and
broken the charm of their invincibility. The news spread far
and wide, and the result of the engagement tended greatly to in-
crease the confidence of the Americans in their own powers, and
impressed them with the idea that they were specially favored by
heaven. Though grieved at the death of their countrymen, yet
the joyful exultation of the Americans was such as well became
the occasion that called it forth.

Gordon's Amer. War, Vol. II, p 39.

(11) CAPT. JOHN CARTER was born in the parish of New Canaan, Conn., and was a man of property and influence, and a
strong friend to his country. He served for a time as captain of
a company, and was engaged in some adventures and skirmishes.
In the month of January, 1780, he commanded a party, which in
conjunction with another party, under Capt. Lockwood, made a
midnight attack upon Col. Hatfield at Morrisania. The affair
was a brilliant one on the part of the Americans, resulting in
the capture of Col. Hatfield, besides one captain, one lieutenant,
one quarter-master, and eleven privates. Captain Carter lived
to an advanced age. He resided after the war in New Canaan,
and died there respected and beloved. His remains were interred in the church-yard at New Canaan.

(12) COWBOYS. This term was applied in the Revolution to an
infamous class of persons who lived between both armies in a
dubious character, being as often in one camp as in the other.
Their occupation was smuggling goods and thieving when op-

portunity afforded. Their propensity for stealing was chiefly exercised on cattle and other live stock, from which circumstance they derived their name.

(13) MAJ.-GEN. CHARLES LEE was a native of Wales. He entered the army at an early age, and served under Gen. Abercrombie, in America, in the campaign of 1758, and four years after under Gen. Burgoyne in Portugal, where he held a colonelcy. In the year 1773 he came to America, and settled in Virginia. On the commencement of the Revolution in 1775, he was appointed Major-General, and repaired with Gen. Washington to the army at Cambridge. He remained there till the following year, when he was ordered to New York to fortify that place, and discharged the duty with great promptness and energy. After this he commanded the Southern forces for a while. In the month of October, 1776, he rejoined the army under Washington, and was soon after captured by the British, and remained a prisoner in their hands till the spring of the year 1778, when he was released and returned to his command. At the battle of Monmouth he was entrusted with a division, and for disobedience of orders, and disrespect to the Commander-in-Chief, on that occasion, he was suspended from his command, and retired to private life. He lived on his farm in Virginia till the year 1782, when he moved to Philadelphia, and died soon after, apparently of chagrin and mortification, at the loss of his reputation, on the 2nd day of October, 1782, at the age of 55 years. He was remarkable for his ability as a writer and for his eccentricity. His military talents were, however, very much overrated.

(14) Governor's Island was known to the Indians by the name of Pagganck, and by the Dutch was called Nooten Eylandt, or Nutting or Nut Island, on account of the abundance of hazel and other nut trees which grew upon it, furnishing the winter's supply

to the citizens. It was called Governor's Island because it was always regarded as a perquisite attached to the office of Governor of the province of New York, and it was cultivated in gardens for their use. Governor Keift had a plantation on the island which he leased for 150 lbs. of tobacco per year.

The island, it is said, was originally so near to Red Hook main land, that cattle crossed the channel to and fro, at low water. Governor's Island was formerly a part of Long Island, being joined to it by a low, intervening morass and a small dividing creek. The widening and deepening of the Buttermilk Channel has been caused by the filling in of the south side of the city.

During the Revolution it was fortified with other islands in the bay of New York, at the time that the City of New York was in anticipation of an attack from Sir William Howe, just after the evacuation of Boston. The island was ceded to the United States by an act of the Legislature of New York, passed Feb. 15, 1800. The grant, however, reserved the right of executing process under the authority of this State. The island is now used solely as a military station of the U. S. Army, and is extensively fortified, and it is supposed would prove of great importance to the defense of the harbor. Its contiguity to the southern part of New York island, makes it an important place of defense, though no fortifications were erected upon it in the early colonial era. It contains about 120 acres of ground, and was at one time used as a race-course.

(15) CAPT. SETH SEYMOUR commanded a company of cavalry during the Revolution, and did considerable service to his country in the course of the war, chiefly in guarding property, and in protecting the sea-coast. He resided in the town of New Canaan, and died there.

(16) The names of the guard who were taken prisoners with

Hanford, on the 13th day of March, 1777, were Wright Everett.
Jonathan Raymond, Samuel Huested, Ebenezer Hoyt. James
Hoyt, Jonathan Kellogg, James Trowbridge, Matthias Com-
stock, Gideon St. John, —— Jarvis, and two others, whose
names cannot, at this time, be ascertained. They all died in
prison, most of them with the small-pox, Ebenezer Hoyt and
Hanford being the only ones who lived to be exchanged. Lieut.
J. B. Eeels, the commander of the guard, was taken prisoner, but
was soon paroled and went home.

The guard were stationed at a hotel kept by Capt. Samuel
Richards. When they were taken prisoners, Capt. Richards was
taken also. The Tories were so embittered against him that they
put him in irons. When the irons were put on his wrists, they
were so hot that the flesh fairly crisped and smoked under the
heat. The blacksmith begged the Tories to let him cool them,
but a Mr. Smith, one of the Tories and a former townsman of
Richards, exclaimed, "*Put them on—it is good enough for the
d—d rebel—let him have it.*" To this Richards replied—"*They
are rather warm, but I can bear them.*"

Mr. Richards was subsequently released on parole, but he vow-
ed vengeance on Smith if he ever met him. At the close of the
war, Smith went with other Tories to Nova Scotia for a place of
refuge, but eventually found his way back to his old home. For
a while he kept himself concealed, and when he went out, ventured cautiously, carefully keeping himself out of the way of Richards. Richards, however, soon ascertained his whereabouts, and
preparing himself for the interview, he went to Smith's hiding-
place, and took him away and settled the matter to his full satis-
faction. How it was adjusted was never known, further than
that Smith was not to be seen for a long time afterwards. Nei-
ther of the parties would ever give any information in regard to
the matter, or as to the mode of settlement, but Richards always

expressed himself satisfied, and Smith appeared to be very glad that the affair was ended.

At the time of the capture of the guard, there was another party taken prisoners with them. This party consisted of Captain Smith, Lieut. Brainard, a d Ensign Bradford. They had been in the service at Horseneck. and their term of duty expired on the 14th. They were discharged on the 13th, and on their way home stopped at Richard's Hotel to stay all night. They were taken with the guard, but were eventually released on parole.

(17) HUNTINGTON. a town of Suffolk Co., Long Island, 45 miles from New York City.

(18) FLUSHING. a town of Queen's County, Long Island, about nine miles from New York City. It has a considerable trade, and its situation is pleasant and healthy. It was settled in 1644 principally by a company of Englishmen, who had been residents of Vissengen. or Flushing. in Holland.

(19) The Middle Dutch Church was erected upon ground purchased by the Consistory in the year 1726, of Mr. David Jamison, for the sum of £575, or about $1,900. The church was opened for divine service in the year 1729, and was used for that purpose until the occupation of the city by the British, when it was first used as a prison and afterwards as a riding-school for the British cavalry. The whole interior of the church was destroyed, leaving nothing but the bare walls and roof. In this desecrated condition the building remained until the year 1788, when repairs were commenced upon it. In the month of July, 1790, it was again re-opened for public worship, on which occasion the Rev. Dr. Livingston preached an interesting discourse. The last sermon preached in the church was on the 11th day of August, 1844.

The building was then leased to the General Government for a Post-Office, and is still occupied for that purpose. It was in the old wooden steeple of this church that Dr. Franklin practised his experiments in electricity.

(20) The Sugar House in Liberty, formerly Crown Street, N. Y., was founded in the year 1689, and was used as a sugar refinery until the year 1776, when it was converted by the British, who then held possession of the city, into a place of confinement for American prisoners. After the Revolution the business of sugar refining was again resumed, and continued until about the month of June, 1840, when the old prison was demolished, and upon its site was erected a block of brick buildings, now used as stores and private offices.

(21 & 22) The first meeting-house, it is said, which was erected in the City of New York, by the Quakers, was built in Green Street Alley, between Liberty Street and Maiden Lane, about the year 1706. It was afterwards moved to Liberty Street, and in the year 1802, was rebuilt and enlarged. It was a plain, substantial building, and stood a little back of the street, on the north side. It was used as a place of meeting, and the grounds attached as a place of burial until after the Yellow Fever of 1822. In the month of October, 1826, the premises were purchased by Grant Thorburn, Esq., and in the month of December following, the ground all around and under the meeting-house, was trenched to the depth of seven feet. The bones were carefully collected, packed in neat boxes, and deposited in a cemetery out of town. In removing the bones, some interesting relics were discovered, among which was a leg and thigh-bone, each of which measured two inches more than any others found there, though there were a great number. They were evidently part of the skeleton of a giant. The building was occupied by Mr. Thorburn

as a seed-store and depot for plants until the year 1835, when the premises were sold by him for building purposes. The old meeting-house was demolished on the 10th day of September, 1835, and upon its site was erected a row of buildings now used as stores and offices.

In the year 1775, the Society of Friends erected a meeting-house in Pearl Street, on the east side, between Cherry and Oak. It was a brick building, 45x68, and covered about 3,264 feet square. It was taken down in the year 1824, and stores and dwelling houses were erected in its place.

These two meeting-houses were both used as hospitals by the British during the Revolution.

Mr. W. B. Hanford believes that the " *Quaker Meeting Hos pital*," in which his father was confined, was the one located in Pearl Street. In regard to the location of the building used as the " *Small-Pox Hospital*," he is less positive. It may have been the meeting-house in Liberty Street, or perhaps have been the First Presbyterian Church in Wall Street, near Broadway, which, it is said, was also used as a hospital. He is, however, not at all certain on this point.

(23) The object of beating the drums at the whipping of the sentinel, was not for the purpose of disgracing him, as is usually the case when the " Rogue's March" is played, but to drown the screeches and groans of the tortured criminal. It answered like-wise as a call, to bring together the regiment to witness the execution of the sentence upon the prisoner.

(24) The Prison Ship Good Intent, on her voyage from England, had been cast upon the rocks at Halifax, whereby she had lost part of her keel. Being unfit for further sea service, she was converted into a prison ship. She required the daily use of her pumps to keep her afloat.]

(25) The Jersey Prison Ship was originally a British ship of the line. She was rated and registered as a 64, but had usually mounted 74 guns. Having become old and decayed, she was, at or near the commencement of the Revolution, dismantled, and soon after moored in the East river, at New York, and used as a store ship. She was afterwards fitted up as a prison ship, and used as such to the termination of the war. In the year 1783, the prisoners then on board of her were released, and she was abandoned where she lay. Her rotted hulk could be seen at low tide for about thirty years afterwards. The mortality on these prison ships was almost incredible. As many as 11,500 are said to have perished on board of them. The remains of those who died in them were slightly buried on the Long Island shore, and the ebbing of the tide often uncovered them, and exposed their whitened bones to view. They were shamefully neglected for many years. In the year 1808, the bones were collected and placed in thirteen coffins, and interred by the Tammany Society in a vault in Jackson Street, Brooklyn, presented for that purpose by the late John Jackson, Esq. A grand imposing procession honored the performance of this last tribute to them.

(26) The Brick Meeting House was erected in the year 1767. It was constructed of brick, and received its name from that circumstance. The celebrated Whitfield is said to have been heard preaching there upon one occasion. The building was 83 feet long by 65 wide, and had a lofty spire. The ground on which it was erected was granted to the church by the corporation of the city, in 1767. There were vaults under the church and in the ground surrounding it, and there was a session room in the rear. In the Revolution the church was used by the British, first as a prison and then as a hospital. It was demolished in the year 1856, and upon its site was erected the elegant edifice known as the "Times Building."

(27) " On a high hill, near where Franklin Street now is, on
the east side of Broadway, there formerly stood a water basin,
built before the Revolution, for supplying the city with water.
Nearly opposite the water basin, on the west side of Broadway,
stood an old fort, built of earth, which had been used during the
Revolutionary war.   On the outside of this fort, on the slope of
the hill, were buried many of the American prisoners of war, who
had died in the old Sugar House in Liberty Street, then Crown
Street, or in the North Dutch Church in William Street, both
of which were used as prisons by the British.   These bodies were
buried so near the surface, that by the slight washing of the hill
their bones were exposed, and many a time, when a boy, have I
seen their remains pulled out and abused by my thoughtless companions—as late as 1800."

Cozzens' Goology of New York Island, page 22.

[Mr. Onderdonk, in speaking of the old Sugar House in Liberty
Street, at the time when it was used as a prison, says : " For
many weeks the dead-cart visited the prison every morning, into
which eight or twelve corpses were flung and piled up, like sticks
of wood, and dumped into *ditches in the outskirts of the city.*"

Onderdonk's Rev. Incidents of Suffolk and Kings Counties, p. 203.

Mr. Jonathan Gillette, a native of West Hartford, Conn., who
died on the 14th day of March, 1855, aged 93 years, was a prisoner in the Sugar House in Liberty Street, in the year 1780,
and was confined there for ten months.   He says, " Almost every
day the corpse of one, and sometimes five or six were carried out
for burial.   They were conveyed to the *Bowery,* near the *Fresh
Water Pump,* where they were interred."

The place where Mr. Hanford witnessed the burial of the prisoners, was not in any church-yard, but was in the trenches of

the fortifications, which had been made by the Americans previous to the evacuation of New York, in the year 1776, in what
was then considered the *upper part of the city*. It was some-
where in the neighborhood of where Grand Street now is, but
may not have been quite so high up. The city was dug full o
trenches, in and around it, and into these the prisoners were
thrown, and were scarcely furnished earth, much less coffins for
their burials. The British did not dig graves for the prisoners,
and hence were not usually inclined to bury them in church-yards
or regular burying places, but threw them in wherever it was
convenient. The mode of burial of those who died in the prison
ships is well known. The remains of those who died in the prisons on land were not more favored than they. During the occupation of the city by the British, much mortality prevailed
among the troops, and the burials said to have been made in
Trinity Church yard, were probably those of British soldiers, or
from the Tory regiments. Mr. Hanford had no knowledge of
any American prisoners having been buried there by the British,
and always scouted at the idea. Having been a prisoner for
fourteen months, he certainly would have known if such had been
the fact. When the troubles with England commenced, the
Episcopal Churches almost unanimously took sides with the mother country, and were friends of the British, and when the City
of New York was taken possession of, they were recognized as
loyal branches of the Established Church of England, and as such
were protected from profanation, while the churches of other de-
nominations were converted into store-houses, hospitals, prisons,
riding-schools, and even stables for British cavalry. The British
being in possession of the Episcopal grounds, they were not at
all likely to desecrate them by making them the receptacle of the
rebel dead. They were not likely to honor or favor those, regarded as criminals and outlaws by a burial in consecrated ground
whom, while living, they had starved and ill treated, and whom

they had allowed to languish and die in vile, pestilential prisons.
The churches themselves were opposed to such burials. They did
not want their grounds filled with the bodies of those who, while
living, were in open rebellion not only against their king, but also
the Established Church. Under these circumstances, the British
certainly would not select such spots when the whole city was
open before them, and would by no means be apt to pay the fee
for interring bodies there, when they could be buried elsewhere
for nothing. If a prisoner had Tory influence enough to insure
his interment there, the same influence would have insured his
release from captivity, and from the treatment and mode of life
which caused or accelerated his decease.

Moreover, Mr. Inglis, the pastor of the church, was himself a
bitter Tory, and took an active and decided part, as is well
known, and as the records of the church will show. He would
have raised both hands against any such desecration. His prayers for the king were vehement and unceasing, and he refused to
omit them even during the presence of Washington himself at
the church, although previously requested so to do by one of that
General's own officers. Would he, who refused this civility to a
member and a communicant of the church, be at all likely to
grant an Episcopal burial to a prisoner confined for being a
rebel, and who died firm and unshaken in his defection? Those
noble patriots, those suffering martyrs were not so favored. No
soothing words consoled their dying hours; no tones of pity soft-
ened their afflictions, and it may well be believed that no Episcopal services attended their remains to their place of interment.

The remains which are said to have been discovered in excava-
ting the ground for the erection of the monument to the Martyrs,
appearing to have been hastily and promiscuously made, and
without coffins, were probably the remains of paupers, for that
ground was used as a Potter's Field for many years before the
Revolution—in fact as early as 1703 or 1704. When the Brit-

ish held possession of the city, they had full control of everything, and is it not natural that they would have protected from desecration the grounds containing their own friends and relatives, and grounds attached to and belonging to their own Established Church? Would not their vigilance after the destruction of the city by fire, in 1776, have been still greater than before? If the grounds were then left more open and exposed, is it at all probable that they would have been less guarded and protected? But one conclusion, therefore, remains, which is, that the remains of those found there *without* coffins were the remains of paupers, while those found there *with* coffins were not the relics of prisoners, for they were uniformly buried without them, and in places not consecrated, and not in the heart of the city, but at *such distances from it* as would prevent the residents from being infected by the effluvia arising from their half-covered bodies while in course of decomposition. During the discussion of these questions, some years ago, Mr. Hanford was referred to, and he always contended that no prisoners were interred by the British in the grounds of that church during the Revolution.

It has been said that the Negro burying ground on the site of Stewart's marble store, corner of Broadway and Chambers Street, and the Jews' burial-ground, on the location now known as Chatham Square, were used as places of interment for American prisoners. Such might have been the case, for the British despised the Jews and their religion, and had no respect whatever for either of those burial-places, and if they buried any prisoners in either of those localities, they did so with the intention of casting a stigma upon them, for they no doubt considered any such interments made by them as an indignity and disgrace.

Before putting this note in type, I sent the manuscript to W. B. Hanford, Esq., for inspection, and with its return received from him the following letter, which I take the liberty to append :—

"FRANKLIN, N. Y., Sept. 21, 1863.

CHAS. J. BUSHNELL, ESQ ,

    My Dear Sir :—Your favor of the 14th instant is before me. * * I have examined the manuscript enclosed, but have no alterations to suggest. It is, I think, correct as it stands, and will give a just view of the facts in relation to the claim of Trinity Church to the honor of furnishing a receptacle for deceased prisoners, and will entitle you to the gratitude of the public for setting the matter right before them.

                Yours, in Fraternal Regards,

                        WM. B. HANFORD."

    (28) The surrender of General Burgoyne took place at Saratoga on the 17th day of October, 1777. It was the cause of great rejoicing on the part of the Americans, who justly considered it as an event having a most important bearing upon the result of the contest between the Colonies and the mother country. The brass artillery captured from Burgoyne at various times during the campaign, amounted to forty-two pieces, constituting one of the most elegant trains ever brought into the field ; five thousand stand of arms ; six thousand dozen cartridges, and a number of ammunition wagons, traveling forges, shot, carcasses, shells, &c., &c., also fell into the hands of the Americans. The whole number of troops surrendered by the convention, amounted to five thousand seven hundred and ninety-two, which, added to the number killed, wounded and captured, in the various actions previous to the 17th of October, amounting to near 5,000, makes Burgoyne's total loss upwards of ten thousand men. He also lost a number of his best officers, among whom were Gen. Fraser and Colonel Breyman. The American army, including 2,500 sick, amounted to 13,200 men.

    The thanks of Congress were voted to General Gates and his army, and a medal of gold, emblematic of the occasion, was presented to him—honors which though bestowed upon him, properly belonged and ought in justice to have been awarded to

Generals Arnold and Morgan, who were the real actors and heroes of the affair, and without whose aid altogether different results might have followed.

General Burgoyne returned to England in the month of May, 1777, where he met with a very cool reception, and was denied admission to the presence of his sovereign. He was even ordered immediately to repair to America as a prisoner, but the ill state of his health prevented compliance. At length he was permitted to vindicate his character. Soon after this, he resigned his emoluments from government, amounting to the sum of $15,000 a year. Towards the close of the year 1781, when a majority of Parliament seemed resolved to persist in the war, he joined in the opposition, and advocated a motion for the discontinuance of the fruitless contest. He knew that it was impossible to conquer America. From the establishment of peace to the time of his death, he lived as a private gentleman, devoted to pleasure and the muses. He published a "Letter to his Constituents," "State of the Expedition from Canada," and some plays which were once very popular, and are considered respectable compositions. Burgoyne was an elegant writer. He died by a fit of the gout, on the 4th day of August, 1792, and nine days after was privately buried in the cloisters of Westminster Abbey.

(29) SERGEANT WALLY was the assistant of William Cunningham, the Provost Marshal. Both of these men were remarkable for their cruelty and inhumanity to the American prisoners, allowing no occasion to pass that afforded them an opportunity to exercise their barbarity. After the war they went to England, and it is said that they both eventually lost their lives upon the scaffold. A confession, said to have been made by Cunningham, in which he acknowledges himself the perpetrator of numerous cold-blooded murders during his official career, was published

many years ago. The names of these two men will be handed down from age to age with undying infamy.

A gentleman, of this city, now in the 89th year of his age, who was present at the evacuation of New York by the British, in 1783, informs me that he lived at that time at the lower end of Murray Street, on the north side of the street. Opposite his residence was a tavern kept by a Mr. Day. An American flag had been hoisted from the tavern before twelve o'clock, the time appointed for the Americans to enter the city, and Cunningham, incensed at the premature display, came there to pull it down. He was met at the door of the tavern by Mrs. Day, a stout, athletic woman, very loyal in her sentiments, who refused him admittance, and upon his attempting to force his way into the house, a scuffle ensued between them, in which she boxed his ears warmly, made the powder fly from his hair, and caused him to beat a hasty retreat, amid the jeers and laughter of some few spectators who were present at the scene. My informant further says that Cunningham was a ruddy-faced Irishman, nearly if not quite six feet in stature. He wore his hair tied in a cue, with powdered bat-wings over his ears. He wore light-colored knee-breeches, and his manner was that of a coarse, insolent and imperious fellow.

(30) EBENEZER HOYT was a member of the same company of cavalry with Levi Hanford, both being under the command of Capt. Seth Seymour. He was taken prisoner with Mr. Hanford, and was confined with him in the Sugar House, and they were the only survivors of the party that was captured. They were liberated together and returned home in company. After regaining his health, Mr. Hoyt again joined the company with Hanford, and continued in the performance of his duty to the end of the war. He lived to an advanced age, and died where he had always lived, in the town of New Canaan.

(31) ELIZABETHTOWN, a town in Essex County, N. J, fifteen miles S. W. of New York City. It is a very thriving place, and has considerable shipping.

(32) NEWARK, a city and seat of justice of Essex Co., N. J., on the Passaic, six miles from Elizabethtown, and nine from New York City. It is handsomely situated, and is particularly noted for producing cider of a superior quality. It is likewise celebrated for its numerous manufactures, among which are carriages, saddlery and harness, boots and shoes, coach lace, chairs, cabinet and plated-ware. Its population in 1848 was 30,000.

(33) DOBBS' FERRY is situated on the Hudson river, twenty-two miles N. of New York, and opposite the northern termination of the Palisades. It was a noted placed during the Revolution.

(34) While Hanford was in prison, his father obtained permission for a flag of truce in order that he might procure the release of his son by exchange for a British officer. On examining the roll of prisoners, it was found that *Levi Sanford* had died in prison some time before. The flag of truce, taking this to mean *Levi Hanford,* reported his death to his friends. This led to the ceremonies and mourning that followed, and caused a suspension of all further efforts towards his release.

(35.) The burning of Norwalk took place in the month of July, 1779. The land forces of the British consisted of about 2,600 men, and were assisted by a fleet of forty armed vessels. The land forces were under the command of Gen. Tryon, assisted by Gen. Garth, an officer of distinguished ability. The troops were landed at New Haven, where they encountered considerable opposition from the inhabitants and militia. After destroying the fort which protected the place, and all the naval and military stores, they proceeded to Fairfield, where the troops were again landed and again opposed. Here the town was set on fire and consumed with everything of value. The same desolation took place at Norwalk, where the militia were more numerous and made greater resistance than at the other places. Here the loss of the Americans was great; both Norwalk and Greenfield, a small town in the neighborhood, were totally destroyed, with a considerable number of ships, either finished or on the stocks, and a still greater number of whale boats and small craft, with stores and merchandize to a large amount. The furniture of the inhabitants was wantonly destroyed, and their plate and other articles of value carried off. One hundred and thirty-two dwelling houses, meeting-house and church included, eighty-seven barns, twenty-two store-houses, seventeen shops, four mills, and five vessels were burnt, besides the wheat and hay, &c., which had been gathered in.

Lendrum's Am. Rev, Vol. II, p. 253.
Bouton's Hist. Discourse, p. 48.

(36) KINGSBRIDGE is situated at the north end of New York island, on Spuyten Duyvel Creek, and is distant from the City Hall about thirteen miles. The neighborhood was the scene of important military operations during the Revolution.

(37) HARTFORD, a city and seat of justice of Hartford Co., Conn., and semi-capital of the State, situated on the Connecticut river, 110 miles from New York City.

(38) FASCINES are made of brush-wood, with their ends sharpened, and are bound together in bundles like sheaves of grain. They are used in forming breastworks, being built in fortifications with dirt, in such a manner that their sharp ends project.

(39) Miss Mary Mead was the daughter of Col. John Mead, and was born at Horseneck, in the town of Greenwich, State of Connecticut, on the 11th day of December, 1759. She was an eye-witness to many acts of cruelty and rapine on the part of the British during our Revolutionary struggle. Her brother, who was an officer in the army, had been taken prisoner and was discharged on parole. He was afterwards exchanged and returned to the army, but becoming sick, was sent home on a furlough. While he was at his home, he heard the British approaching the house and fled from the back door, and under the protection of an orchard, made his way to the fields, where he sprang into a thicket and hid himself. While he lay here concealed, a party of British Light Horse surrounded the house, and some of them coming up to his sister Mary, who had gone to a neighboring spring to rinse some clothes, pointed their swords at her breast and threatened her with instant destruction, unless she revealed the hiding-place of her brother. By her presence of mind and firmness on this occasion, she not only saved her own life but also preserved his.

At another time the house was surrounded by a party of British Light Horsemen, and one of them struck at her twin-sister with his sword, just missing her head, but cutting the casing of the door, an inch in thickness, quite in two. The family were repeatedly plundered by marauding parties of their clothes and other valuable effects. They would carry off everything of value, and what they could not take away, they would destroy. They would even ride into the house, and upset the chairs and tables, and hack to pieces with their swords, mirrors, pictures and furniture. They would rip open the feather beds, and empty into the ticks hives of bees with the honey. The family were compelled to secrete their clothing and valuable effects in the fields and other places of security to preserve them from pillage.

After the termination of the war, Miss Mead was married to

Levi Hanford. In the year 1809, she and her husband united
with the Baptist Church in Franklin, Delaware County, N. Y.,
then under the pastoral charge of Rev. Daniel Robertson, and
to the close of their lives lived in Christian fellowship with the
church, and evinced by their conduct, in public and private, the
sincerity of their belief in the religion they professed. Mrs.
Hanford died at Walton, Delaware County, N. Y., on the fifteenth day of September, 1847, in the eighty-eighth year of her
age, and was buried in the family cemetery at that place.

(40) COL. JOHN MEAD was born in Greenwich, Connecticut,
in the year 1726, and was a farmer by occupation. Being a very
fleshy man, his farm labor was mostly performed by his sons and
hired help. He was at one time connected with the building of
several vessels, one of which was taken in the early part of the
Revolution by the British. He was placed early in command
of the American lines at Horseneck, together with an extent of
sea-coast each way from that place. He had command of a
regiment, and sent out men by companies, or in smaller detach-
ments, as he had orders, or as he deemed the public safety de-
manded. He was with his regiment at the evacuation of the
City of New York, under General Washington, and his regiment
was the last to leave the place. The day was a remarkably
warm and sultry one, and the men suffered greatly from heat and
thirst, and many of them were sun-struck. Col. Mead remained
after the regiment had left, and before he had overtaken his men,
they had retreated to a place of safety. When he entered the
public house, he found every spot occupied. Even the floor was
covered promiscuously with officers and men, seeking repose and
sleep after the labors of the day. Edging his way along, he at
length found a place, and stretched himself upon the floor among
them. Incommoding, however, one of his neighbors, by using
his feet for a pillow, the man remonstrated, when the Colonel

immediately apologized. The soldier recognized the voice of his commander and exclaimed :

" Why, Colonel Mead—is it you ? God bless you ! Can it be possible you are alive and well? I really never expected to see you again alive after what we have endured. Lie down, Colonel, —use my feet for a pillow, and welcome, if you can find any rest in such a place."

On one occasion, while the Colonel was at his home at Horse-neck, a party of British and Tories formed a plan to capture him for the purpose of exchanging him for one of their officers who had been taken by the Americans some time before. The party set out from Long Island, and were piloted along by a man who had been brought up by the Colonel, and who was dependent upon him, and whom he had often befriended. When the Colonel saw this man among the party, he at once exclaimed,

" Eben, I hardly expected such treachery at your hands."

The only reply he received was,

" Colonel, you know times have changed."

The party were pursued but succeeded in effecting their escape to Long Island with their prisoner. On their arrival at their place of destination, they offered the Colonel a parole, which he declined. He was, however, soon after exchanged.

The farm and residence of Colonel Mead being situated in the forepart of the American lines, was a constant place of resort by the Tories and Cowboys, who committed so much depredation, and annoyed the family to such a degree, that they were finally compelled to leave the place and move to New Canaan, some fifteen or twenty miles distant, to avoid further persecution.

At the termination of the war, they returned to their home, but found it to be a mere wreck of what it had once been. The roofs of the houses had been torn off, the windows broken in, the doors and ceilings destroyed, and some of the walls demolished. Fences had been pulled down and used for fire-wood, the farming utensils and implements had been carried off or destroyed, and the stock upon the farm had been killed or driven off by Cowboys. The Colonel found himself reduced from a good and valuable estate to limited means and straightened circumstances. His native State, however, made up for some of his losses, by a grant of a large tract of land in that part of Ohio, owned at that time by Connecticut, and known as the " Connecticut Fire Lands." The people of his locality honored him by making him their representative to the Legislature for nineteen consecutive years, and up to the time of his death. He was also promoted to the rank of Brigadier General.

He died of dropsy in the year 1788, in the sixty-third year of his age, and was interred in the burying-ground at Horseneck. His wife's maiden-name was Mary Brush. She was of Scotch extraction, and was born in Stanwix, a parish of Greenwich, State of Connecticut. She died several years prior to the death of her husband, at the age of about forty years.

(41) HORSENECK, a village in Fairfield County, Connecticut, noted for the defeat of the Indians by the Dutch in the year 1646.

[42) GREENWICH a town in Fairfield County, Conn. The settlement was begun after it had been purchased of the Indians, in 1640, under the Dutch Government at New York, then New Amsterdam. In 1665 it was incorporated by Governor Stuyvesant. It was, however, originally purchased for the Colony of New Haven by Robert Feeks and Daniel Patrick. But the purchasers violated their engagements to that Colony, and together with the few inhabitants, placed themselves under the government of New Amsterdam. The settlement went on very heavily until the people returned to the jurisdiction of Connecticut, then including the Colony of New Haven. The Indians were hostile to the Dutch, and were not very favorably inclined towards the inhabitants. "A great and general battle was fought between them in that part of Horseneck commonly known by the name of Strickland's Plain. The action took place in 1646, and was long and severe, both parties fighting with much obstinacy. The Dutch with much difficulty kept the field, and the Indians withdrew. Great numbers were slain on both sides, and the graves of the dead, for a century or more, appeared like a number of small hills." The population in 1850 was 5,040.

(43) New Canaan, a town of Fairfield County, Conn., incorporated in 1801. It was originally a parish lying partly in Stamford and Norwalk, and was incorporated as a parish in 1731. Its business consists chiefly in leather manufacture. Its population in 1850 was 2,601.

(44) The town of Walton in Delaware County, was organized about the year 1793. The first frame house erected in the town was built by Robert North, who afterwards became the first supervisor. There being no saw mills near, the boards and timber were floated down the river from Paine's mill at Hobart. The wife of Mr. North often boasted that she was the first woman that ever made a foot-print upon the soil of Walton. The first grist-mill was erected in 1793, and the first wedding in the town took place in 1790. Many of the early settlers of the town emigrated from New Canaan, in Connecticut. The population in 1841 was about 2,000.

Gould's Hist. Delaware County.

(45) Peter St. John was born in Norwalk, Conn., about the year 1762. Though he was too young to take a part in the commencement of the war, yet he rendered some service to his

country before its close as a volunteer.   He moved to Walton,
N. Y., in the year 1802 with his family.   He became a professor
of religion, and gave much time and labor to the study of the
Scriptures.   This with a happy communication, gave him an influence in the Congregational Church to which he belonged,
which has outlived the man.   Early on his arrival in Walton, he
was elected Deacon of the church, which office he retained to the
close of his life.   He was a farmer by occupation, and possessed
a competency, and was elected by his townsmen to discharge the
duties of several public offices.   He was in the course of his life
the husband of three wives, and he was the father of six sons.
He lived to an advanced age, and died as he lived, a man respected and beloved.